THE COOK': ✳ 'ON

POULTRY
& SMALL GAME

Author: Annette Wolter

Photography: Susi and Pete Eising, Odette Teubner,
   Rolf Feuz and Karin Messerli

Translated by UPS Translations, London

Edited by Josephine Bacon

CLB 4153
This edition published in 1995 by Grange Books
an imprint of Grange Books PLC, The Grange, Grange Yard, London SE1 3AG
This material published originally under the series title "Kochen Wie Noch Nie"
by Gräfe und Unzer Verlag GmbH, München
© 1995 Gräfe und Unzer Verlag GmbH, München
English translation copyright: © 1995 by CLB Publishing, Godalming, Surrey
Typeset by Image Setting, Brighton, E. Sussex
Printed and bound in Singapore
All rights reserved
ISBN 1-85627-755-0

THE COOK'S COLLECTION
✳
POULTRY
& SMALL GAME

Annette Wolter

Grange BOOKS

Introduction

The many benefits of eating poultry instead of other meats are now well established. Dieticians tell us that it is a healthy food that is high in protein and low in fat. It is also tender, easy to digest, and versatile. Poultry readily absorbs other flavours and can be combined with virtually anything – a plain and simple dish one day, and a roast fit for royalty the next. Poultry meat is extremely tasty and generally suits everyone, as it is relatively inexpensive and widely available in a variety of cuts. We can choose from the whole, ready-to-cook bird, breast fillets, legs, thighs, halves, quarters, and diced or minced portions. It is a very convenient food.

In these pages you will find a selection of delicious recipes for chicken, duck, goose and turkey, covering a wide range of possibilities from simple, tasty soups and salads to luxurious main dishes. Some game birds, such as pheasant, are also included in this selection. Game birds are becoming more readily available in many butchers and supermarkets. However, if you cannot obtain any such bird, chicken can always be substituted as long as you remember to extend the cooking time accordingly.

Poultry must always be thoroughly cooked. To ensure that a bird is properly cooked through, pierce the thigh with a skewer to see if the juices run clear. If there is any sign of blood, cook it for a little longer.

Enjoy experimenting with this selection of exciting new recipes, and prepare to be surprised by the wide variety of flavours they offer.

Each recipe serves four, unless otherwise indicated

Lemon Soup with Chicken

1 onion
15g/¹/₂oz butter
300g/10oz chicken breast
1l/1³/₄ pints chicken stock
8 tbsps par-boiled rice
Salt and freshly ground white pepper
1 pinch freshly grated nutmeg
3 eggs
Juice of 1 lemon
Approximately 12 leaves lemon balm

Preparation time:
30 minutes
Nutritional value:
Analysis per serving, approx:
• 1200kJ/290kcal
• 29g protein
• 12g fat
• 19g carbohydrate

fine strips. Brown the meat by frying it with the onions. Add the chicken stock and bring to the boil. • Add the rice to the soup and simmer gently for 5 minutes. Season with salt, pepper and nutmeg. •Whisk the eggs with the lemon juice. • Remove the soup from the heat and stir in the whisked egg. • Wash and dry the lemon balm. • Preheat soup bowls. Serve the soup sprinkled with the lemon balm.

Peel the onion and chop finely. • Melt the butter in a large saucepan and fry the chopped onion until transparent. • Wash the chicken, pat dry and cut into

Duck Soup with a Pastry Lid

250g/8oz duck breast
1 tsp sunflower oil
Salt and freshly ground white
pepper
2 spring onions
250g/8oz courgettes
100g/4oz mushrooms
750ml/1¼ pints chicken stock
150g/5oz veal sausage meat
2 tbsps finely chopped fresh
chervil
4 tbsps double cream
4 sheets frozen rough puff
pastry, thawed
1 egg yolk

Preparation time:
40 minutes
Cooking time:
15 minutes
Nutritional value:
Analysis per serving, approx:
• 2300kJ/550kcal
• 25g protein
• 36g fat
• 32g carbohydrate

Wash and dry the duck breast. Heat the oil, and fry the duck, skin side down, until browned. Turn and fry for a further 3 minutes or until cooked. Remove from the pan and drain on kitchen paper. Season to taste with salt and pepper. • Trim, wash and slice the spring onions. Wash, pat dry and dice the courgettes. Wash, pat dry and slice the mushrooms. • Place the chicken stock in a pan and bring to the boil. • Mix together the sausage meat, chervil and 2 tbsps of cream, and season to taste with pepper. Using a damp teaspoon, shape dumplings from the mixture. Add the dumplings to the stock, and simmer for 10 minutes. • Slice the duck breast into matchstick strips and divide between two large soup bowls. Divide the spring onions, courgettes and mushrooms between the bowls. • Roll out the dough on a lightly floured surface into circles 2cm/3/4 inch larger than the diameter of the bowls. Beat the egg yolk with the remaining cream. • Fill the bowls with the hot soup and the dumplings. Lay the dough

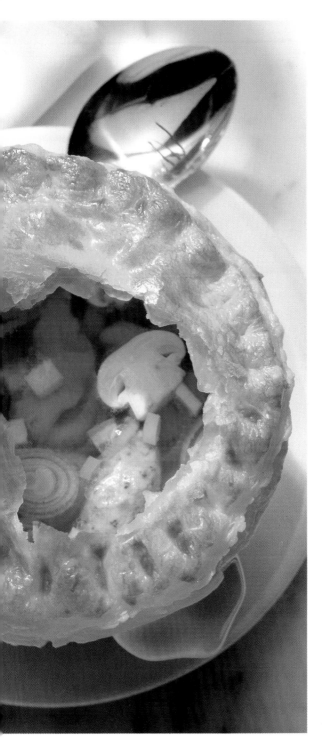

circles over the tops of the
bowls, and seal the edges.
Brush the surface of the dough
with the egg yolk and cream
mixture. • Bake in a preheated
oven at 220°C/425°F/gas
mark 7 for about 15 minutes,
or until the pastry has risen and
is golden.

9

Hungarian Chicken Soup

750g/1lb 8oz chicken pieces
100g/4oz carrots
2 celery stalks
100g/4oz cauliflower
1 garlic clove
1 beefsteak tomato
1 onion
1 sprig parsley
6 black peppercorns
Salt
50g/2oz French beans
50g/2oz shelled peas
50g/2oz vermicelli

Preparation time:
30 minutes
Cooking time:
1¼ hours
Nutritional value:
Analysis per serving, approx:
• 2500kJ/600kcal
• 41g protein
• 39g fat
• 23g carbohydrate

Wash the chicken pieces and pat dry. Peel the carrots and cut half of them into matchstick strips, leaving the others whole. Cut 1 celery stalk into matchstick strips. Cut the other in half. • Wash the cauliflower and divide into florets. • Peel the garlic. Quarter the tomato. Peel and roughly chop the onion. • Place the chicken pieces in a pan, cover with cold water and bring to the boil. • Add the whole carrots and halved celery stalk, garlic, tomato, onion, parsley and peppercorns, and season to taste with salt. Bring to the boil again, lower the heat and simmer for 1 hour. Skim frequently during this time. • Slice the beans. Add the carrot and celery strips, cauliflower florets, beans and peas to a pan of lightly salted boiling water, cover and cook for 10 minutes. Drain. • Cook the vermicelli in 500ml/16 fl oz boiling water for 3 minutes and drain. • Skin the chicken and cut the meat from the bones. Dice the chicken meat and place in a tureen. Add the vermicelli, carrot strips, celery strips, cauliflower, peas and beans. • Strain over the stock, and discard the stock vegetables. Serve the soup immediately.

Polish Pheasant Soup

1 x 1kg/2¼lbs pheasant
1.5l/2½ pints water
6 black peppercorns
1 bay leaf • Salt
2 carrots • 1 leek
3 tbsps sunflower oil
1 tbsp wholemeal flour
125ml/4fl oz crème fraîche
2 tbsps finely chopped fresh parsley

Preparation time:
45 minutes
Cooking time:
1½ hours
Nutritional value:
Analysis per serving, approx:
• 2300kJ/550kcal
• 55g protein
• 35g fat
• 10g carbohydrate

Wash the pheasant. Place in a pan, add the water, peppercorns and bay leaf, and season with salt to taste. Bring to the boil and cook over a high heat for 1 hour. • Peel and slice the carrots. Trim and wash the leek and slice into thin rings. • Remove the cooked pheasant from the stock and set aside. Remove and discard the bay leaf. Rub the stock through a sieve. • Heat the oil in a pan, and fry the carrots and leek, stirring constantly, until lightly coloured. Add the flour and cook, stirring constantly, for 3 minutes or until golden. Gradually stir in the vegetable stock. Bring to the boil, lower the heat and simmer for 10 minutes. • Skin the pheasant and cut the meat from the bones. Dice the meat. • Add to the soup and heat through. Remove from the heat, and stir in the crème fraîche. • Serve the soup sprinkled with the parsley.

Chicken Liver Terrine

To serve 6:

600g/1¼ lbs chicken livers
175g/6oz thinly sliced rindless bacon
2 thyme sprigs
2 rosemary sprigs
2 onions
25g/1oz dried ceps
½ tsp dried thyme
½ tsp dried rosemary
½ tsp ground cloves
½ tsp ground cinnamon
½ tsp ground mace
½ tsp ground ginger
5 tbsps medium sherry
Salt
500g/1lb 2oz minced veal or sausagemeat
200ml/7fl oz crème fraîche
2 tbsps finely chopped fresh parsley
3 bay leaves
2l/3½ pints boiling water

Preparation time:
1 hour
Cooking time:
45 minutes
Nutritional value:
Analysis per serving, approx:
• 3080kJ/735kcal
• 35g protein
• 60g fat
• 7g carbohydrate

Trim and wash the chicken livers and pat dry. • Reserve 4 slices of the bacon and finely dice the remainder. Wash the thyme and rosemary sprigs, shake dry and set aside. Peel and finely chop the onions. • Heat a small pan, and fry the diced bacon until the fat runs. Add the onions, and fry until transparent. Add the chicken livers, and stir-fry for 3 minutes until lightly browned. Add the ceps, dried

12

thyme, dried rosemary, cloves, cinnamon, mace, ginger and sherry, and season to taste with salt. Fry for a further 1 minute, stirring constantly. Remove from the heat and set aside to cool. • Roughly chop the livers. Mix together the chopped livers, the veal or sausagemeat, crème fraîche and chopped parsley. Season to taste with salt. • Spoon the mixture into an ovenproof terrine or loaf tin and smooth the top. Place the thyme and rosemary sprigs and the bay leaves on top of the mixture and cover with the reserved bacon slices. • Cover with a double layer of aluminium foil and seal the edges. Place in a large ovenproof dish or roasting tin. Add enough boiling water to come halfway up the sides of the terrine or loaf tin. • Cook in a preheated oven at 175°C/350°F/ gas mark 4 for 45 minutes. • Remove from the oven and set aside to cool. Serve in slices or scoop out with a spoon. • Accompany with Cumberland sauce and freshly-baked baguette.

Savoury Toppers

To make 25:
200g/7oz turkey or chicken livers
1 onion
25g/1oz butter
Sea salt and freshly ground black pepper
3 tbsps double cream
½ tsp finely chopped fresh thyme
½ tsp finely chopped fresh marjoram
2 tsps finely chopped fresh parsley
7 cherry tomatoes
25 fresh basil or marjoram leaves

For the Crackers:
200g/7oz wholemeal flour
Pinch curry powder
Pinch mild paprika
½ tsp baking powder
Salt and freshly ground white pepper
100g/4oz butter
1 egg
2 tbsps sesame seeds

Preparation time:
45 minutes
Baking time:
10 minutes
Nutritional value:
Analysis per cracker, approx:
• 340kJ/81kcal
• 3g protein
• 5g fat
• 5g carbohydrate

Sift the flour with the curry powder, paprika, baking powder and a pinch of salt and pepper. Dice 100g/4oz of the butter, and distribute around the edge of the flour. Break the egg into the flour. Mix to a dough with your hands, pulling the ingredients from the outside. Shape the dough into a roll 5cm/2 inches across and 15cm/6 inches long. Trim and chop the livers. Peel and finely chop the onion. • Melt half the butter, and fry the onion until lightly browned. Add the livers, cover, and fry for 5 minutes. Season, and set aside to cool. • Purée the cooled livers with the frying juices, cream, thyme and marjoram. Stir in the parsley, and season. • Grease a baking sheet with the remaining butter. • Cut the roll of dough into 5mm/¼ inch slices, and

14

place on the baking sheet. Sprinkle over the sesame seeds and press down gently. Bake in a preheated oven at 200°C/400°F/gas mark 6 for 10 minutes until golden. • Transfer to a wire rack, and set aside to cool. • Spread the crackers with the paste, and garnish with the tomatoes and basil or marjoram.

Goose in Aspic

To serve 6:

1 x 3kg/6¾ lb goose, with giblets
500g/1lb 2oz veal bones
2 onions
4 red peppers
2 carrots
2 celery stalks
Peel 1 lemon
1 bay leaf
2 cloves
4 peppercorns
½ tsp dried thyme
Pinch dried basil
Pinch dried tarragon
Salt
500ml/16fl oz vinegar
1.75l/3 pints boiling water
1 bouquet garni
45g/1½ oz powdered gelatine
Bunch of curly parsley

Preparation time:
1 hour
Cooking time:
2 hours
Setting time:
4 hours

Nutritional value:
Analysis per serving, approx:
• 5290kJ/1260kcal
• 60g protein
• 98g fat
• 3g carbohydrate

Separate the drumsticks from the goose. Cut the body into 4 pieces. Wash the goose pieces, giblets and veal bones. • Peel and chop the onions. Halve, seed, wash and dice the peppers. Peel the carrots. Trim and halve the celery stalks. • Place the goose pieces, giblets, veal bones, onions, peppers, carrots and celery in a large pan. Add the lemon peel, bay leaf, cloves, peppercorns, thyme, basil and tarragon, and season to taste with salt. Pour over the vinegar. • Cover with boiling water and bring to the boil. Skim several times. Lower the heat, cover and simmer for 1 hour. • Add the bouquet garni, and simmer for a further 1 hour. • Remove the goose pieces, carrots and celery and

set aside. • Strain the stock, and set aside to cool. Skim off the fat. • Skin the goose pieces and cut the meat from the bones. Dice the meat. • Slice the carrot, and cut the celery into matchstick strips. • Sprinkle the gelatine onto a small bowl of hot water. Set aside for 5 minutes to soften. Heat 5 tbsps of the reserved stock in a pan. Stir the gelatine, and add to the hot stock, in a continuous stream, stirring constantly. Add the remaining stock, stir and season to taste with salt and pepper. Set aside to cool. • Wash the parsley and shake dry. Pull off the leaves and discard the stalks. • Rinse out a large mould with cold water, and pour in a thin layer of aspic. Put the aspic in the refrigerator to set. • Arrange some parsley and a few vegetable slices over the aspic. Cover with a further layer of aspic, and return to the refrigerator to set. • Make a second layer of goose meat,

vegetables and parsley, cover with aspic and return to the refrigerator to set. Continue making layers in this way until all the ingredients are used up. • Finally, return to the refrigerator for a further 4 hours or until completely set. • Before serving, loosen the edge of the aspic from the bowl using a sharp, heated knife. Plunge the bowl briefly into hot water and turn out the aspic onto a plate. • Can be served with roast potatoes and sweet and sour salad made from beetroot or wax beans.

Chicken Croissants

To make 10:
400g/14oz skinless chicken
fillets
200g/7oz mushrooms
2 onions
50g/1oz butter
1 tsp dried thyme
Salt and freshly ground white
pepper
2 tbsps double cream
1 egg
1 tbsp condensed milk
5 sheets frozen rough puff
pastry, thawed

Preparation time:
1 hour
Baking time:
20 minutes
Nutritional value:
Analysis per croissant, approx:
• 800kJ/190kcal
• 12g protein
• 11g fat
• 12g carbohydrate

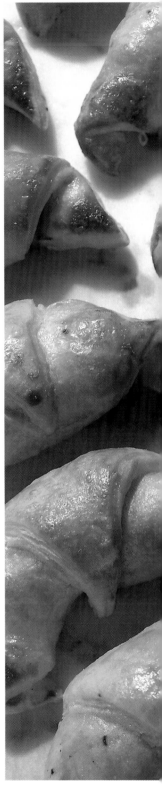

Wash the chicken fillets
and pat dry. Finely dice.
Finely chop the mushrooms.
Peel and finely chop the
onions. • Melt the butter, and
fry the onions until
transparent. Add the
mushrooms, and thyme, and
season to taste with salt and
pepper. Cook, stirring
frequently, until the liquid has
evaporated. Remove the
mixture from the heat, stir in
the cream and set aside to cool.
• Separate the egg. Stir the egg
white and the chopped
chicken into the mushroom
mixture. • Beat together the
egg yolk and the condensed
milk. • Rinse a baking sheet
with cold water. • Cut the
pastry sheets in half diagonally,
and roll out each triangle
widthways on a lightly floured
work-surface. Divide the filling
among the triangles, and roll
up from the long side. Bend
into croissant shapes. Brush the
croissants with the egg yolk
and condensed milk mixture

and place on the baking sheet.
• Bake in a preheated oven at
200°C/400°F/gas mark 6 for
20 minutes until golden.

18

Sweet and Sour Goose Pieces

250g/8oz mixed dried fruit
salad
1kg/2¼lbs goose pieces
750ml/1¼ pints water
1 onion
2 cloves
1 bay leaf
1 bouquet garni
Salt and freshly ground black
pepper
50g/2oz butter
5 tbsps flour
2 tbsps vinegar
1 tbsp sugar

Soaking time:
12 hours
Preparation time:
25 minutes
Cooking time:
1½ hours
Nutritional value:
Analysis per serving, approx:
• 3100kJ/740kcal
• 23g protein
• 48g fat
• 57g carbohydrate

Place the dried fruit in a bowl, cover with cold water and leave to soak for 12 hours. • Wash the goose pieces. Place the goose pieces and water in a pan, bring to the boil and skim. • Peel the onion and stud with the cloves. Add the onion, cloves, bay leaf and the bouquet garni to the pan, and season to taste with salt. Cover and cook over a low heat for 30 minutes. Add the dried fruit and its soaking liquid, cover, and cook for a further 30 minutes. The stock should reduce by at least one third during the cooking time. • Remove the goose pieces and the dried fruit from the stock and set aside. Remove the bouquet garni and discard. Rub the stock through a sieve and reserve 500ml/16fl oz. • Melt the butter, and stir in the flour. Cook, stirring constantly, for 3 minutes or until golden. Gradually stir in the reserved stock and simmer for 10 minutes, stirring occasionally. • Stir in the vinegar and sugar, and season to taste with salt and pepper. • Add the dried fruit and the goose pieces, and heat through. • Dumplings make an excellent accompaniment.

Pörkölt Chicken

To serve 6:
1 x 1.5kg/3lbs 6oz chicken, with giblets
2l/3½ pints water
1 bouquet garni
Salt and freshly ground white pepper
100g/4oz rindless streaky bacon
4 onions
2 green peppers
2 beefsteak tomatoes
1 tbsp sunflower oil
2 tbsps paprika

Preparation time:
1 hour
Cooking time:
2 hours
Nutritional value:
Analysis per serving, approx:
• 3400kJ/810kcal
• 50g protein
• 63g fat
• 9g carbohydrate

Wash the chicken and the giblets. Set aside the liver, and place the chicken and the remaining giblets in a pan. Add the water and the bouquet garni, and season. Bring to the boil, skim, lower the heat and simmer for 1½ hours. • Dice the bacon. Peel and chop the onions. Halve, core, seed and wash the peppers. Cut into matchstick strips. Skin the tomatoes and cut into wedges. • Remove the chicken and the giblets from the stock. Divide the chicken into 12 pieces and dice the giblets. Remove the bouquet garni and discard. Rub the stock through a sieve and reserve 500ml/16fl oz. • Heat the oil, and fry the bacon until the fat begins to run. Add the chicken pieces, and fry until golden on all sides. Add the onions and peppers, and fry until the onions are lightly coloured. Stir in the paprika. • Place the reserved stock in a pan. Add the chicken pieces, onions, peppers and giblets, and cook for 10 minutes. • Chop the reserved chicken liver. Add the liver and tomatoes to the pan, and simmer for a further 10 minutes. Season to taste.

Fruity Cock-a-Leekie

1 x 1kg/2¼lbs chicken
1 chicken heart
10 prunes
1 onion
6 tbsps pearl barley
Salt and freshly ground black pepper
800g/1½lbs leeks
1 chicken liver
2 tbsps finely chopped fresh parsley

Preparation time:
40 minutes
Cooking time:
1½ hours
Nutritional value:
Analysis per serving, approx:
• 2300kJ/550kcal
• 59g protein
• 18g fat
• 44g carbohydrate

Wash the chicken. Place the chicken, chicken heart and the prunes in a pan, and add enough water just to cover. Bring to the boil and skim. Lower the heat. • Peel and finely chop the onion. Add the onion and pearl barley to the pan, and season to taste with salt and pepper. Cover and poach over a very low heat for 1¼ hours. The surface of the water should be barely rippling. • Trim and wash the leeks and cut into rings. • Add the leeks and the chicken liver to the pan, and cook for a further 15 minutes. • Remove the cooked chicken and giblets from the stock. Skin the chicken and cut the meat from the bones. Thinly slice the meat and giblets. • Return the pan to fairly high heat and boil vigorously until the stock has reduced by one third. • Add the chicken meat and giblets, and heat through. Season to taste with salt and pepper. • Serve sprinkled with the parsley.

Paella

To serve 8:
1 x 1.2kg/2½lbs chicken
250g/8oz pork fillet
Salt and freshly ground black
pepper
6 tbsps olive oil
500g/1lb 2oz mussels
300g/10oz long-grain rice
2 onions
2 garlic cloves
750ml/1¼ pints chicken stock
125ml/4fl oz dry white wine
1/2 tsp saffron
100g/4oz shelled peas
200g/7oz smoked garlic
sausage or Spanish chorizo
6 cooked king prawns
4 beefsteak tomatoes
1 lemon
100g/4oz black olives

Preparation time:
2 hours
Nutritional value:
Analysis per serving, approx:
• 2625kJ/625kcal
• 51g protein
• 31g fat
• 36g carbohydrate

Rinse the chicken and pat dry. Cut into 12 pieces. Wash, pat dry and dice the pork. • Season the chicken and pork with salt and pepper to taste. • Heat 4 tbsps of the oil in a large pan, and fry the chicken pieces until golden on all sides. Add the pork, and fry until lightly coloured. Lower the heat and cook the chicken and pork for a further 20 minutes, stirring frequently. • Scrub the mussels under cold running water, discarding any that do not close when sharply tapped. Pull off the beards. • Rinse the rice under cold running water. • Thinly slice the sausage. Add to the pan, and fry until lightly coloured. • Peel and finely chop the onions and garlic. Heat the remaining oil in another large pan, and fry the onions and garlic until lightly coloured. Add the rice and fry, stirring constantly, until golden. Pour over the chicken stock and wine. Stir in the saffron. Cook the rice for 10 minutes over a

24

low heat. • Add the peas, and cook for a further 10 minutes. Skin the tomatoes and cut into 8. • Transfer the rice to a paella pan or a large, flat, ovenproof dish. Arrange the chicken, pork, mussels, sausage, prawns and tomato wedges on top. • Bake in a preheated oven at 200°C/400°F/gas mark 6 for 20 minutes. • Cut the lemon into wedges. • Switch off the oven and leave the paella to rest for 5 minutes. Scatter over the olives. Garnish with the lemon wedges and serve immediately.

Our tip: *Paella is made in many different ways in Spain, depending on the region and the availability of ingredients. If you can bring a typical smoked chorizo sausage back from Spain, you can make an authentic paella.*

Chicken in Apricot Sauce

1 large onion
500g/1lb 2oz apricots
1 x 1.2kg/2½ lb chicken
6 tbsps sunflower oil
2 tbsps flour
About 375ml/15fl oz hot
water
2 tsps caster sugar
Salt and freshly ground white
pepper

Preparation time:
40 minutes
Cooking time:
30 minutes
Nutritional value:
Analysis per serving, approx:
• 2300kJ/550kcal
• 64g protein
• 25g fat
• 26g carbohydrate

Peel and finely chop the onion. Wash the apricots in lukewarm water. Dry, halve and stone. • Wash the chicken and pat dry. Cut into 8 pieces. • Heat the oil, and fry the chicken over a medium heat until browned on all sides.

Remove from the pan. •
Reserve 1 tbsp of the oil and discard the remainder. •
Return the pan to a low heat, and stir in the flour. Gradually stir in sufficient hot water to form a thick sauce. • Stir in the onion, and cook over a low heat for 3 minutes, stirring frequently. Stir in the apricots and sugar, and season to taste with salt and pepper. Place the chicken pieces in the sauce. •
Cover and braise over a low heat for a further 30 minutes. •
This dish may be served with brown rice or mashed potato and any type of salad.

Chicken Drumsticks with Mushrooms

8 chicken drumsticks
4 tbsps flour
1 onion
1 garlic clove
15g/½oz butter
4 tbsps olive oil
1 tbsp tomato purée
100ml/3½fl oz dry red wine
Pinch dried marjoram
Pinch dried thyme
Salt and freshly ground white
pepper
1 bunch parsley
350g/11oz mushrooms
Juice ½ lemon
1 tbsp wine vinegar

Preparation time:
40 minutes
Cooking time:
30 minutes
Nutritional value:
Analysis per serving, approx:
• 2200kJ/520kcal
• 66g protein
• 22g fat
• 13g carbohydrate

Wash the chicken drumsticks and pat dry. Toss in the flour to coat completely. • Peel and chop the onion and garlic. • Melt the butter with 1 tbsp of the oil, and fry the drumsticks, onion and garlic until the chicken is browned on all sides. • Mix together the tomato purée, wine, marjoram and thyme, and season to taste with salt and pepper. Add to the pan, and cook for 30 minutes. • Wash the parsley and shake dry. Reserve a few sprigs for the garnish and chop the remainder. • Finely slice the mushrooms, and sprinkle with the lemon juice. • Heat the remaining oil in another pan, and fry half the chopped parsley and the mushrooms until all the liquid has evaporated. • Add the mushrooms to the chicken drumsticks. Sprinkle with the vinegar and the remaining parsley. • Transfer to a serving dish and garnish with the reserved parsley sprigs.

Turkey Roll with Soft Cheese

2 carrots
1 small onion
40g/1½ oz butter
2 tbsps finely chopped fresh
mixed herbs
100g/4oz full-fat soft cheese
1 egg yolk
1 tbsp French mustard
Salt and freshly ground white
pepper
2 x150g/5oz turkey escalopes
250ml/8fl oz hot chicken stock
4 tbsps dry vermouth
2 tbsps crème fraîche

Preparation time:
30 minutes
Cooking time:
20 minutes
Nutritional value:
Analysis per serving, approx:
• 1600kJ/380kcal
• 39g protein
• 22g fat
• 7g carbohydrate

Peel the carrots and cut into matchstick strips. Peel and finely chop the onion. • Melt 15g/½oz of the butter, and fry the carrot and onion over a low heat for 5 minutes. Set aside to cool slightly. • Mix together the herbs, cheese, egg yolk and mustard, and season to taste with salt and pepper. • Wash the turkey and pat dry. Spread the cheese and herb mixture evenly over the escalopes. Divide the onion and carrots between them. Roll up the escalopes and secure with wooden cocktail sticks. • Melt the remaining butter, and fry the escalopes over a medium heat until browned on all sides. Pour over the stock and vermouth. Cover and cook over a low heat for 20 minutes. • Transfer the turkey rolls to a carving dish or chopping board and remove the cocktail sticks. Cut the rolls into slices, transfer to a serving dish and keep warm. • Stir the crème fraîche into the cooking juices and heat through. Serve the turkey with new potatoes and carrots and hand the sauce separately.

Turkey Rolls with Vegetables

50g/2oz raisins
100g/4oz raw ham
1 onion
3 tbsps finely chopped fresh parsley
2 tbsps pine nuts
1 tbsp capers
4 x 150g/5oz turkey escalopes
Salt and freshly ground white pepper
4 tbsps olive oil
4 tbsps tomato purée
125ml/4fl oz water
200ml/7fl oz single cream
1 small bay leaf
1 tsp finely chopped fresh rosemary
½ tsp dried thyme
1 red pepper
Pinch of sugar

Preparation time:
45 minutes
Nutritional value:
Analysis per serving, approx:
• 2400kJ/570kcal
• 42g protein
• 37g fat
• 16g carbohydrate

Place the raisins in a small pan. Cover with water and bring to the boil. Drain. • Dice the ham. Peel and finely chop the onion. • Mix together the raisins, ham, parsley, pine nuts and capers. • Wash the turkey escalopes and pat dry. Season to taste with salt and pepper. Divide the ham and raisin mixture between the escalopes, roll up and secure with wooden cocktail sticks. • Heat the oil, and fry the onion and turkey rolls until the rolls are browned on all sides. Add the tomato purée, water, cream, bay leaf, rosemary and thyme. Cover and cook over a low heat for 20 minutes. • Halve, seed and wash the pepper. Cut into strips. Add to the pan, and cook for a further 10 minutes. Stir in the sugar. • Transfer to a serving dish, remove the cocktail sticks and serve immediately.

29

Breast of Pheasant in Bacon

2 x 1kg/2¼ lbs pheasants
Salt and freshly ground white
pepper
1 tsp dried sage
40g/1½ oz butter
50g/2oz very thinly sliced
rindless streaky bacon
250g/8oz sweet chestnuts
2 tsps sugar

Preparation time:
1 hour
Nutritional value:
Analysis per serving, approx:
• 3300kJ/790kcal
• 81g protein
• 42g fat
• 31g carbohydrate

Wash the pheasants and pat dry. Rub the insides with salt and pepper. Crush half the sage, and divide between the insides of the pheasants. • Melt 25g/1oz of the butter, and fry the pheasants for 5 minutes until browned all over. • Place, breast side up, in a roasting tin. Pour over the melted butter and wrap in the bacon slices. Roast in a preheated oven at 220°C/425°F/gas mark 7 for 30 minutes. Remove from the oven, transfer to a dish and set aside to cool. • Using a small, sharp knife, cut a cross in the pointed ends of the chestnuts, place in a pan and cover with water. Bring to the boil and cook for 20 minutes. • Rinse the chestnuts in cold water and peel. • Melt the remaining butter in a pan, add the sugar, and cook gently, stirring constantly, until the sugar has dissolved. Coat the chestnuts in the mixture to glaze and set aside to cool. • Cut the breast from the pheasants and carve into 1cm/½ -inch thick slices, together with the bacon. Arrange on a serving dish with the chestnuts and sprinkle over the remaining sage. (Use the remaining pheasant meat in other recipes.)

Chicken Breast with Kiwi Fruit

800g/1½ lbs chicken breast
1 l/1¾ pints chicken stock
1 leek
1 celery stalk
4 kiwi fruit
1 orange
1 lemon
15g/½ oz butter
1 tbsp sugar
Pinch cayenne
Salt

Preparation time:
45 minutes
Nutritional value:
Analysis per serving, approx:
• 1300kJ/310kcal
• 49g protein
• 5g fat
• 21g carbohydrate

Wash the chicken breast. Place the chicken stock in a pan and bring to the boil. Add the chicken, and cook for 10 minutes, skimming frequently. • Trim, wash and slice the leek. Trim, wash and slice the celery. Add to the stock, lower the heat and poach for a further 10 minutes. The surface of the water should be barely rippling. • Peel the kiwi fruit and cut into 5mm/1/4 -inch slices. Arrange the kiwi fruit on a serving dish. • Wash the orange in hot water and dry. Thinly pare half the peel from the orange. Cut the peel into thin strips and set aside. • Squeeze the lemon and the orange. • Melt the butter in a small pan, add the sugar, and cook gently, stirring constantly, until the sugar has dissolved. Stir in the fruit juice, bring to the boil and allow to reduce to about 2 tbsps of liquid. Add the cayenne pepper, and season to taste with salt. Allow to cool and pour over the kiwi fruit. • Skin and bone the chicken breast. Carve into slices and arrange on the kiwi. Sprinkle with the reserved orange peel.

Chicken Livers with Lentils

1l/1¾ pints water
350g/11oz red lentils
100g/4oz raw ham
500g/1lb 2oz chicken livers
50g/2oz butter
1 tbsp olive oil
3 tbsps finely chopped fresh parsley
1 tbsps finely chopped fresh sage
3 tbsps chicken stock
Salt and freshly ground black pepper
1 sage sprig

Preparation time:
40 minutes
Nutritional value:
Analysis per serving, approx:
• 1800kJ/430kcal
• 38g protein
• 25g fat
• 13g carbohydrate

Bring the water to the boil. Add the lentils, and cook over a low heat for 8 minutes. Drain. • Finely dice the ham. Wash the chicken livers and pat dry. Trim and cut into strips. • Melt half the butter with the oil in a pan, and fry the ham, parsley and sage over a low heat, stirring constantly, for 5 minutes. Add the stock, cover, and cook for a further 5 minutes. • Melt the remaining butter in another pan, and stir-fry the chicken livers for 3-4 minutes. Season to taste with salt and pepper. Mix together the lentils, ham mixture and chicken livers. Transfer to a serving dish and garnish with the sage leaves. Serve immediately. • Mashed potato or freshly baked baguette make an excellent accompaniment.

Light Chicken Fricassée

1 x 1.5kg/3lb 6oz chicken
2 onions
1 bouquet garni
1 bay leaf
1 tsp black peppercorns
1l/1¼ pints water
Salt and freshly ground white pepper
50g/2oz butter
125ml/4fl oz dry white wine
250ml/8fl oz double cream
100g/4oz crème fraîche
200g/7oz carrots
150g/5oz celery
1 small leek
½ tsp dried tarragon
1 tbsp finely chopped fresh parsley

Preparation time:
30 minutes
Cooking time:
1 hour
Nutritional value:
Analysis per serving, approx:
• 3200kJ/760kcal
• 58g protein
• 49g fat
• 21g carbohydrate

Separate the drumsticks and breast from the chicken. Thinly slice and set aside. Cut the remaining parts into several pieces. Peel the onions and finely chop 1, leaving the other whole. • Place the chicken pieces, but not the breast and drumsticks, in a pan, and add the bouquet garni, bay leaf, the whole onion, peppercorns and water, and season to taste with salt. Bring to the boil, lower the heat and simmer for 30 minutes. The liquid should reduce by about one quarter. • Rub the chicken stock through a sieve and reserve. (Use the meat in another recipe.) • Wash the chicken breast and drumsticks and pat dry. Halve and rub with the pepper. Melt the butter, and fry the breast and drumsticks until golden brown. Add the remaining onion, and fry for 5 minutes. Add the chicken stock and wine, and cook for 30 minutes. The liquid should reduce by half. • Stir in the cream and crème fraîche, and reduce by half. • Peel the carrots and cut into matchstick strips. Trim and wash the celery and cut into matchstick strips. Trim, halve and wash the leek and cut into matchstick strips. • Stir the carrots, celery, leek, tarragon and parsley into the pan, and simmer for 3 minutes.

Chicken in Tarragon Sauce

2 garlic cloves
1 x 1.2kg/2½ lb chicken
4 tbsps olive oil
2 bay leaves
Juice 1 lemon
250ml/8fl oz dry white wine
4 tbsps tarragon vinegar
Salt and freshly ground white pepper
1 tbsp chopped fresh tarragon
12 black olives, to garnish
1 tbsp coarsely chopped peanuts

Preparation time:
20 minutes
Cooking time:
40 minutes
Cooling time:
1 hour
Nutritional value:
Analysis per serving, approx:
• 2400kJ/570kcal
• 62g protein
• 33g fat
• 5g carbohydrate

Peel and finely chop the garlic. Wash the chicken and pat dry. Cut into 8 pieces. • Heat the oil, and fry the chicken pieces until browned all over. Add the garlic and the bay leaves, and stir-fry until the onion is lightly browned. Sprinkle over the lemon juice. Add the wine and vinegar, and season to taste with salt and pepper. Bring to the boil. Lower the heat, cover, and simmer for 40 minutes, turning the chicken pieces frequently. • Remove the chicken and set aside. • Bring the cooking juices to the boil and allow to reduce. Set aside to cool. • Arrange the chicken pieces on a plate, drizzle over the cold cooking juices and sprinkle over the tarragon. Serve garnished with the olives and chopped peanuts.

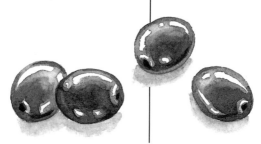

Chicken with Anchovy Mayonnaise

1 x 1.2kg/2½ lb chicken
1 bunch parsley
3 basil sprigs
1 bouquet garni
1 onion
1 clove
1 bay leaf
100g/4oz canned tuna, drained
4 anchovy fillets
1 tbsp capers
1 gherkin
4 tbsps mayonnaise
1 tsp lemon juice
Salt and freshly ground white pepper
1 lemon
Lettuce leaves, to garnish

Preparation time:
30 minutes
Cooking time:
1½ hours
Cooling time:
2 hours
Nutritional value:
Analysis per serving, approx:
• 2300kJ/550kcal
• 71g protein
• 30g fat
• 3g carbohydrate

Wash the chicken and place in large pan. •

Wash the parsley, remove the leaves and set aside, reserving the stalks. Wash the basil sprigs and add to the pan, together with the bouquet garni and reserved parsley stalks. Peel and halve the onion. Stud one half of the onion with the clove and place both onion halves and the bay leaf in the pan. Cover with boiling water. • Cook the chicken for 30 minutes, skimming frequently. Lower the heat, and poach the chicken for a further 1 hour. The surface of the water should be barely rippling. • Remove from the heat and set aside to cool in the stock. • Finely chop the tuna, anchovy fillets, capers and gherkin, and mix together. Stir the anchovy mixture into the mayonnaise. Add the lemon juice, and season to taste with salt and pepper. Finely chop the parsley leaves, and stir into the anchovy mayonnaise. • Remove the chicken from the pan, skin and cut the meat from the bones. Slice the meat and arrange on a serving dish. Cut the lemon into wedges. • Serve with the anchovy mayonnaise and garnish with the lemon wedges and lettuce leaves.

Chicken Curry

*500g/1lb 2oz chicken breast
fillets
½ bunch spring onions
1 large beefsteak tomato
½ pineapple
25g/1oz butter
1 tsp flour
2 tbsps curry powder
250ml/8fl oz chicken stock
1 tsp lemon juice
Salt*

Preparation time:
30 minutes
Nutritional value:
Analysis per serving, approx:
• 1100kJ/260kcal
• 30g protein
• 7g fat
• 21g carbohydrate

Wash the chicken and pat
dry. Cut into strips
about 1cm/½ inch wide. •
Trim and wash the spring
onions. Cut the pale green
parts into 1cm/½-inch rings.
Cut the white ends lengthways

into quarters. • Skin and dice
the tomato. • Peel, quarter,
core and slice the pineapple •
Melt the butter, and fry the
chicken until golden brown.
Add the onions and tomato,
and fry for a further 1 minute.
• Mix together the flour and
curry powder, and stir into the
pan. Gradually stir in the stock.
• Add the pineapple, and
simmer over a low heat for 5
minutes. Stir in the lemon
juice and season to taste with
salt. • This fruity curry may be
served with brown rice.

Chicken Breast with Walnuts

500g/1lb 2oz chicken breast
fillets
3 tbsps soya sauce
2 tbsps dry sherry
½ tsp sugar
2 tbsps cornflour
Salt
1 red pepper
1 onion
200g/7oz celery
5 tbsps corn oil
100g/4oz shelled walnuts
125ml/4fl oz hot chicken stock

Preparation time:
35 minutes
Nutritional value:
Analysis per serving, approx:
• 1800kJ/430kcal
• 34g protein
• 25g fat
• 14g carbohydrate

Wash the chicken and pat dry. Cut into 2cm/¾ - inch cubes, and place in a shallow dish. • Mix together the soya sauce, sherry, sugar and cornflour, and season to taste with salt. Pour the mixture over the chicken. • Halve, seed and wash the pepper and cut into matchstick strips. Peel the onion and cut into matchstick strips. Trim and wash the celery and cut into matchstick strips. • Heat 1 tbsp of the oil, and fry the walnuts until pale brown. Remove from the pan. • Add 1 tbsp of the remaining oil, and stir-fry the celery for 1 minute. Add the onion, and stir-fry for 1 minute. Add the pepper, and stir-fry for 1 minute. Remove the vegetables from the pan. • Heat the remaining oil, and stir-fry the chicken for 3 minutes. Lower the heat and add the stock. Return the vegetables and walnuts to the pan and heat through. • Transfer to a serving dish and serve with rice.

Duckling with Olives

1 x 1.6kg/3lb 10oz duckling
1 onion
1 garlic clove
2 tbsps small capers
3 tbsps olive oil
3 tbsps finely chopped fresh parsley
2 tbsps torn fresh basil leaves
Salt and freshly ground black pepper
100ml/3fl oz dry white wine
125ml/4fl oz chicken stock
2 duck livers
250g/8oz stoned green olives

Preparation time:
45 minutes
Cooking time:
1 hour
Nutritional value:
Analysis per serving, approx:
• 4700kJ/1100kcal
• 79g protein
• 84g fat
• 5g carbohydrate

Wash the duckling and pat dry. Cut into 8 pieces. • Peel and finely chop the onion and garlic. Finely chop the capers. • Heat the oil in a flameproof casserole, and fry the duckling until browned all over. Reduce the heat, and add the onion, garlic, capers, parsley and basil. Fry for about 10 minutes, stirring frequently. Season to taste with the salt and pepper. • Add the wine, and cook over a low heat, stirring constantly, until the liquid has evaporated. Add the stock, cover, and simmer for about 50 minutes. • Wash the livers, pat dry, trim and finely chop. Stir the olives and livers into the casserole, cover and simmer for a further 10 minutes. • Serve with white bread and tomato salad.

Duckling with Tomatoes

1 x 1.6kg/3lb 10oz duckling
2 rosemary sprigs
6 black peppercorns
100ml/3½fl oz dry white wine
100ml/3½fl oz wine vinegar
1 large onion
600g/1¼ lbs ripe tomatoes
4 tbsps olive oil
Pinch saffron
Salt and freshly ground black
pepper
5 tbsps chicken stock

Marinating time:
3 hours
Preparation time:
40 minutes
Cooking time:
1 hour
Nutritional value:
Analysis per serving, approx:
• 4200kJ/1000kcal
• 75g protein
• 77g fat
• 9g carbohydrate

Wash the duckling and pat dry. Cut into 8 pieces, and place in a large shallow dish. • Add the rosemary, peppercorns, wine and vinegar, and set aside to marinate for 3 hours, turning from time to time. • Peel and thinly slice the onion and push out into rings. Skin and roughly chop the tomatoes. • Heat the oil in a flameproof casserole, and fry the onion until golden brown. Add the tomatoes and saffron, and season to taste with salt and pepper. Cover and cook for 15 minutes. • Remove the duckling from the marinade and drain. Add the duckling and stock to the casserole, cover and simmer for 1 hour. Add a little more chicken stock if necessary. • Adjust the seasoning, if necessary • Serve the dish with rice and a green salad.

Duckling in Pineapple Sauce

1 x 1.5kg/3lb 6oz duckling
1 tbsp corn oil
125ml/4fl oz pineapple juice
250ml/8fl oz dry red wine
Juice 1 lemon
Salt and freshly ground white pepper
1 tbsp cornflour
Juice and finely grated peel 1 orange
1 fresh pineapple
1 tbsp pineapple conserve or low-sugar jam

Preparation time:
25 minutes
Cooking time:
1 hour
Nutritional value:
Analysis per serving, approx:
• 2860kJ/680kcal
• 46g protein
• 44g fat
• 17g carbohydrate

Wash the duckling and pat dry. Cut into 6 pieces and sprinkle with the oil. Place in a roasting tin, and cook in a preheated oven at 200°C/400°F/gas mark 6 for 20 minutes. • Mix together the pineapple juice, wine and lemon juice, and season to taste with salt and pepper. Pour over the duckling, return to the oven and roast for a further 1 hour, basting frequently. • Mix together the cornflour and orange juice to make a smooth paste. • Peel, quarter, core and slice the pineapple. Cut into chunks. • Remove the duckling from the roasting tin and keep warm. • Skim the fat from the cooking juices, then rub the juices through a sieve. Set over a low heat. Stir in the cornflour mixture and bring to the boil, stirring constantly. Stir in the orange peel and, if necessary, a little water. Add the pineapple slices and the pineapple conserve or jam, and season to taste with salt and pepper. • Transfer the duckling to a

serving dish and pour over the
sauce. • This is especially tasty
served with glazed sweet
potatoes.

41

Turkey and Tomatoes

2 x 600g/1¼ lb turkey
drumsticks or thighs
2 garlic cloves
1 tsp finely chopped fresh
rosemary
Salt and freshly ground white
pepper
3 tbsps wine vinegar
5 canned anchovy fillets,
drained
1 x 400g/14oz can tomatoes
3 tbsps olive oil
1 tbsp capers
2 egg yolks
Juice ½ lemon
15g/½oz butter

Marinating time:
2 hours
Preparation time:
30 minutes
Cooking time:
1¼ hours
Nutritional value:
Analysis per serving, approx:
• 2100kcal/500kcal
• 70g protein
• 22g fat
• 6g carbohydrate

Wash the turkey and pat
dry. Peel and finely
chop the garlic, and mix with
the rosemary. • Rub the
turkey with salt, pepper and
the garlic and rosemary
mixture and place in a shallow
dish. Pour over the vinegar,
cover and set aside to marinate
for 2 hours, turning the turkey
several times. • Finely chop the
anchovy fillets. Partially drain
the tomatoes and coarsely
chop. • Remove the turkey
from the marinade. Heat the
oil, and fry the turkey until
golden brown all over. Add
the anchovy fillets. Stir in the
tomatoes and capers, cover and
cook for 1¼ hours. Add a little
tomato can juice if necessary. •
Remove the turkey from the
pan. Skin and cut the meat
from the bones. Cut into
3cm/1½-inch cubes. Return
the meat to the pan to heat
through. • Beat together the
egg yolks and lemon juice. Stir
the egg yolk mixture and the
butter into the pan. Transfer to
a serving dish and serve
immediately.

Turkey Escalopes with Coriander

250g/8oz shallots
1 garlic clove
4 x 150g/5oz turkey escalopes
4 tbsps oil
½ tsp crushed coriander seed
Salt and freshly ground white
pepper
1 x 400g/14 oz can tomatoes
1 tsp chicken stock granules
½ tsp sugar
¼ tsp cayenne pepper
1 tbsp coarsely chopped fresh
parsley

Preparation time:
40 minutes
Nutritional value:
Analysis per serving, approx:
• 1100kJ/260kcal
• 36g protein
• 10g fat
• 9g carbohydrate

Peel the shallots and garlic. Wash the escalopes and pat dry. • Heat the oil, and stir in the coriander. Season the escalopes to taste with salt and pepper. Add to the pan, and fry over a high heat for 1 minute on each side. Remove from the pan. • Add the shallots, and fry until golden brown. Crush the garlic and add to the pan. • Drain the tomatoes, and add the juice to the pan. • Coarsely chop the tomatoes. Add the tomatoes, stock granules, sugar and cayenne pepper to the pan, and cook, stirring, until the mixture has thickened. • Return the escalopes and any meat juices to the pan. Cover and cook over a low heat for 5 minutes. • Sprinkle over the parsley, transfer to four individual plates and serve immediately. • This is delicious served with noodles.

Turkey Wings with Peaches

750g/1½ lbs turkey wings
(about 3 wings)
1 small bay leaf
1 bouquet garni
3 white peppercorns
Salt and freshly ground black
pepper
2l/3½ pints water
200g/7oz tagliatelle
750g/1½lbs ripe peaches
50g/2oz butter
1 tbsp finely chopped fresh dill
1 tbsp snipped chives

Preparation time:
30 minutes
Cooking time:
1 hour
Nutritional value:
Analysis per serving, approx:
• 2400kJ/570kcal
• 47g protein
• 18g fat
• 55g carbohydrate

Wash the turkey wings and pat dry. Place in a pan and add the bay leaf, bouquet garni and peppercorns. Add salt to taste and sufficient water just to cover. Cover and simmer for 1 hour. • Bring the water to the boil. Add a pinch of salt and the tagliatelle, and cook for about 10 minutes or until tender but still firm to the bite. Drain. • Skin, halve and stone the peaches. Cut into slices. • Melt the butter, and stir-fry the peaches for 5 minutes. • Remove the turkey wings from the stock and set aside to cool slightly. • Skin the turkey wings and cut the meat from the bones. Cut the meat into pieces and season to taste with salt and the pepper. • Mix together the noodles, peach slices and turkey and reheat. • Transfer to a serving dish, sprinkle over the dill and chives and serve immediately.

Pheasant with Bacon Sauce

1 x 1.2kg/2½ lb pheasant,
with giblets
Salt and freshly ground black
pepper
8 thin slices rindless bacon
50g/2oz butter
1 carrot
150g/5oz leeks
2 tbsps sunflower oil
2 tbsps finely chopped fresh
parsley
2 crushed juniper berries
5 peppercorns
500ml/16fl oz water
125ml/4fl oz grape juice
3 tbsps dry sherry
125ml/4fl oz crème fraîche

Preparation time:
40 minutes
Cooking time:
40 minutes
Nutritional value:
Analysis per serving, approx:
• 4200kJ/1000kcal
• 65g protein
• 78g fat
• 12g carbohydrate

Wash the pheasant and pat dry. Cut off the wings. Rub the inside of the pheasant with salt and pepper. • Wrap the breast in half the bacon slices. • Melt the butter in a roasting tin, and fry the pheasant until browned all over. • Roast the pheasant, breast side down, in a preheated oven at 220°C/425°F/gas mark 7 for 30 minutes. • Remove the bacon and discard. Turn the pheasant over and roast for a further 10 minutes to brown the breast. • Dice the remaining bacon. Peel and finely chop the carrot. Trim, halve, wash, and thinly slice the leek. • Heat the oil, and fry the bacon. Add the pheasant wings and giblets, and fry until lightly browned. Add the carrot, leek, parsley, juniper berries, peppercorns and water, and season to taste with salt and pepper. Bring to the boil. Lower the heat, cover and simmer for 20 minutes. • Discard the wings. Rub the sauce through a sieve. • Transfer the pheasant to a serving dish and keep warm. • Place the sauce and roasting juices in a small pan over a medium heat. Stir in the grape juice and the sherry, bring to the boil and allow to reduce to 250ml/8fl oz. Stir in the crème fraîche.

Braised Pigeon in Chocolate Sauce

2 garlic cloves
4 x 500g/1lb 2oz pigeons
Salt and freshly ground white pepper
3 tbsps flour
4 tbsps olive oil
4 tbsps dry white wine
250ml/8fl oz chicken stock
200g/7oz shallots
50g/2oz cooking chocolate

Preparation time:
40 minutes
Cooking time:
50 minutes
Nutritional value:
Analysis per serving, approx:
• 2200kJ/520kcal
• 54g protein
• 29g fat
• 17g carbohydrate

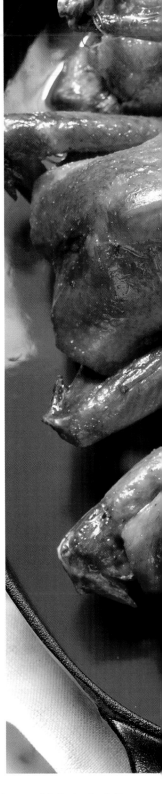

Peel and finely dice the garlic. • Wash the inside and outside of the pigeons. Rub the inside and outside with salt and pepper, and coat with 2 tbsps of the flour. • Heat the oil in a large flameproof casserole, and fry the pigeons until golden brown all over. Remove from the casserole. • Add the garlic to the casserole, and fry until just beginning to colour. • Stir in the remaining flour, and cook, stirring constantly, for 1 minute. Gradually stir in the wine and the chicken stock, and cook for 5 minutes, stirring constantly. • Return the pigeons to the casserole, cover, and cook over a low heat for 30 minutes. • Peel and finely dice the shallots. Add the shallots to the casserole, cover and cook for a further 20 minutes. • Transfer the pigeons to a serving dish and keep warm. • Skim the fat off the sauce. Grate the chocolate. Stir into the sauce over a low heat until it has melted. Do not allow the sauce to boil. Season to taste with salt and pepper. Serve the pigeons with

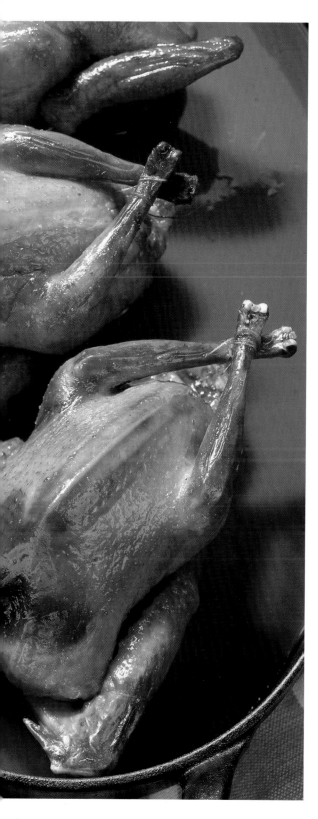

the sauce. • This is delicious
with brown rice or a fresh
baguette and a mixed fresh
salad.

Sesame Chicken

1 onion
50g/2oz sesame seeds
25g/1oz butter
2 tbsps sesame oil
2 tsps cracked wheat
Salt and freshly ground white
pepper
1 egg
1 tbsp finely chopped fresh
parsley
1 x 1kg/2¼ lb chicken

Preparation time:
30 minutes
Cooking time:
1 hour
Nutritional value:
Analysis per serving, approx:
• 2200kJ/520kcal
• 57g protein
• 33g fat
• 6g carbohydrate

Peel and finely chop the onion. Dry-fry half the sesame seeds. Melt half the butter with half the oil in the pan with the sesame seeds. Add the onion and cracked wheat, and stir-fry until the onion is lightly browned. Remove from the heat. Season to taste with salt and pepper, and allow to cool slightly. Stir in the egg and parsley. • Rinse the chicken and pat dry. Spoon in the stuffing and close with trussing thread. • Season the remaining sesame seeds to taste with salt and pepper, and rub into the chicken. • Melt the remaining butter with the remaining oil. Brush the chicken with half the butter and oil mixture. Place the chicken, breast side down, in a roasting tin and roast in a preheated oven at 220°C/425°F/gas mark 7 for 25 minutes. Turn and roast for a further 25 minutes. • Brush the chicken with the remaining butter and oil mixture and roast for a further 10–15 minutes, basting frequently with the roasting juices. • Turn off the heat and leave the chicken to rest in the hot oven for 10 minutes.

Barbecued Chicken with Mango Butter

100g/4oz butter
1 tbsp mango chutney
Juice ½ lime
Pinch cayenne
1 x 1.5kg/3lb 6oz chicken
2 tbsps sunflower oil
Salt and freshly ground white pepper

Preparation time:
30 minutes
Cooling time:
1 hour
Cooking time:
30 minutes
Nutritional value:
Analysis per serving, approx:
• 3000kJ/710kcal
• 77g protein
• 50g fat
• 1g carbohydrate

Beat the butter to soften. Mix together the butter, mango chutney, lime juice and cayenne pepper. Form the mango butter into a roll. Wrap in aluminium foil or greaseproof paper, and place in the freezer for 2 hours to set. • Wash the chicken and pat dry. Cut into 8 pieces, brush with half the oil and season to taste with salt and pepper. • Cook under a preheated hot grill for 30 minutes, turning at least twice and brushing with the remaining oil from time to time. • Cut the chilled mango butter into 8 equal slices and place on the hot chicken pieces. • Serve with curried rice salad, fresh pita bread and an avocado and tomato salad, or sliced, ripe mango.

Our tip: *Alternatively the chicken pieces can be cooked on a barbecue.*

Traditional Christmas Goose

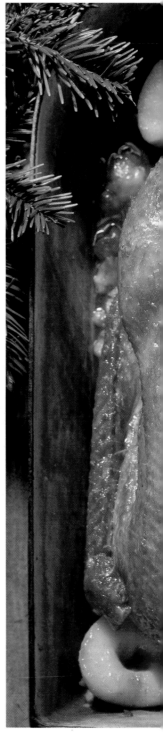

To serve 8:
750g/1½ lbs sweet chestnuts
500ml/16fl oz chicken stock
1 x 5kg/11lb 4oz goose
Salt and freshly ground pepper
500g/1lb 2oz cooking apples
100g/4oz raisins
½ tsp dried sage
250ml/8fl oz boiling water
2 tsp cornflour
½ tsp sugar

Preparation time:
1 hour
Cooking time:
4 hours
Nutritional value:
Analysis per serving, approx:
• 6870kJ/1635kcal
• 76g protein
• 124g fat
• 58g carbohydrate

Cut a cross in the chestnuts and roast in a preheated oven at 180°C/350°F/gas mark 4 until the skins burst. Cool slightly then peel. • Bring the chicken stock to the boil. Add the chestnuts and boil for 10 minutes. Drain and allow to cool. • Rinse the goose and pat dry. Rub with salt and pepper. • Peel, core and slice the apples. Wash the raisins and pat dry and mix with the chestnuts, apples and sage. Spoon the stuffing into the goose and truss. • Place the goose, breast side down on a rack over a roasting tin. Pour the boiling water into the tin, and roast the goose in a preheated oven at 180°C/350°F/gas mark 4 for 1 hour. • Turn the goose over and pierce the skin of the drumsticks so that the fat can run out. Roast the goose for a further 2½ hours. • Brush with cold, salted water to crisp the skin and return to the oven for a further 30 minutes. • Transfer the goose to a serving dish, and keep warm. • Skim the fat from the roasting juices. Dilute the roasting juices with a little hot water and strain. Make up to 500ml/16fl oz with water. Set over a medium heat and bring to the boil. Mix together the cornflour and 2

50

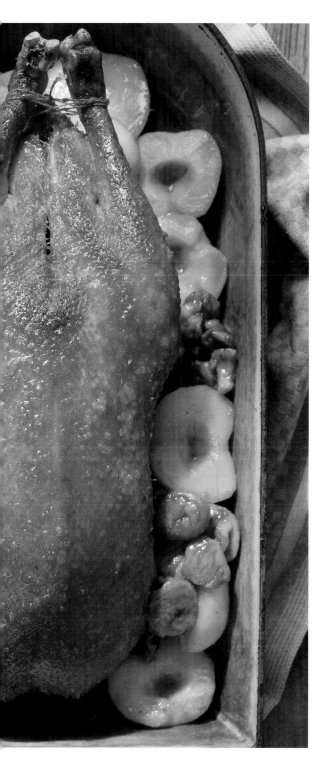

tbsps cold water to make a smooth paste. Stir the paste into to the roasting juices. Cook, stirring constantly, until thickened. Stir in the sugar, and season to taste with salt and pepper. • Serve the goose and hand the sauce separately.

51

Quail with Truffle Stuffing

4 quails
Salt and freshly ground white
pepper
200g/7oz goose livers
40g/1½ oz butter
2 tbsps Madeira
2 tsps bottled truffle pieces
1 tbsp finely chopped fresh
basil
2 tbsps dry breadcrumbs
½ head endive
2 small seedless mandarins
2 tbsps orange juice
1 tbsp olive oil
2 basil sprigs

Preparation time:
1¼ hours
Nutritional value:
Analysis per serving, approx:
• 2940kJ/700kcal
• 34g protein
• 59g fat
• 12g carbohydrate

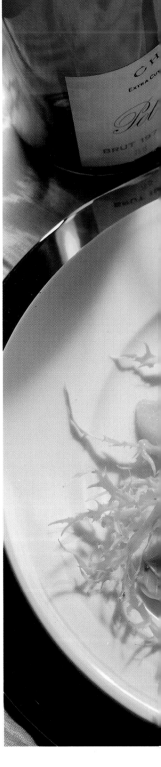

Wash the quails and pat
dry. Rub the inside with
salt and pepper. • Wash the
goose livers and pat dry. Trim
and dice. • Melt 15g/½oz of
the butter, and stir-fry the
livers until lightly browned.
Add 1 tbsp of the Madeira, and
season to taste with salt and
pepper. Cook, stirring
constantly, for 5 minutes.
Remove the pan from the
heat. • Finely chop the truffles.
Mix together the liver, truffles,
chopped basil and
breadcrumbs. • Spoon the
stuffing into the quails and
close with trussing thread. •
Melt the remaining butter in a
roasting tin over a medium
heat, and fry the quails until
browned all over. Roast in a
preheated oven at
200°C/400°F/gas mark 6 for
20 minutes. Transfer to a
serving dish, remove the
trussing thread and set aside to
cool. • Wash, shake dry and
shred the endive. Peel the

mandarins, divide into
segments and remove the
membrane. • Mix together the
orange juice, remaining
Madeira and olive oil, and
season to taste with salt. Mix

together the endive and
mandarins, pour over the
dressing and toss lightly. •
Arrange on the serving dish
with the quails and garnish
with the basil sprigs.

Stuffed Turkey Fillet

To serve 8:
400g/14oz spinach
2 onions
2 garlic cloves
1 thick slice stale bread, crusts removed
2 tbsps olive oil
50g/2oz freshly grated Parmesan cheese
50g/2oz cream cheese
1 egg
2 tbsps breadcrumbs
2 tbsps flaked almonds
½ tsp dried oregano
Pinch of ground nutmeg
Salt and freshly ground black pepper
1.5kg/3lbs 6oz turkey breast in one piece
½ tsp dried thyme
4 tbsps sunflower oil
125ml/4fl oz boiling water
200g/7oz mushrooms
2 shallots
15g/½ oz butter
2 tbsps finely chopped fresh parsley
250ml/8fl oz double cream
250ml/8fl oz crème fraîche

Preparation time:
1 hour
Cooking time:
1½ hours
Relaxing time:
6 hours
Nutritional value:
Analysis per serving, approx:
• 2500kJ/600kcal
• 54g protein
• 35g fat
• 16g carbohydrate

Trim and wash the spinach. Place in a pan and cook for 5 minutes in the water still clinging to the leaves. Drain, squeeze out excess water and finely chop. • Peel and chop the onions. Peel and finely chop the garlic. • Tear the bread into pieces and place in a bowl. Cover with cold water and set aside to soak. • Heat the olive oil, and fry the onion and garlic for 5 minutes or until transparent but not browned. Add the spinach, and stir-fry until all the liquid has evaporated. Transfer to a bowl. • Squeeze out the bread. Mix together the spinach, Parmesan

cheese, cream cheese, egg, breadcrumbs, flaked almonds, oregano and nutmeg, and season to taste with salt and pepper. • Wash the turkey breast and pat dry. Using trussing thread, sew up the places in the meat where the bones were removed. Cut a deep pocket in the meat and spoon in the spinach stuffing. Sew the meat together with trussing thread. • Rub with salt and pepper, sprinkle over the thyme and place in a roasting tin. • Heat the sunflower oil, and pour over the turkey. Roast in a preheated oven at 200°C/400°F/ gas mark 6 for 1½ hours, frequently pouring a little hot water around the turkey and basting the meat with the roasting juices. • Remove the turkey from the roasting tin and wrap in foil. When cold, set aside in the refrigerator to rest for 6 hours. • Make the sauce. Thinly slice the mushrooms. Peel and finely chop the shallots. • Melt the butter, and stir-fry the mushrooms for 3 minutes over a high heat. Add the shallots and parsley, and stir-fry until browned. Season with salt and pepper to taste and remove from the heat. Stir in the cream and crème fraîche. Transfer to a sauce boat, cover and set aside in the refrigerator. • Remove the turkey from the foil and take out the trussing thread. Carve the turkey in thick slices and hand the sauce separately.

Duck and Mushroom Pie

Makes 1 x 26cm/8-inch pie
To serve 12:
2.5l/4½ pints water
Salt and freshly ground white
pepper
1 x 2kg/4½ lb duck, with
giblets
1 onion
2 cloves
1 bouquet garni
½ bay leaf
100g/4oz mushrooms
60g/2½oz butter
3 tbsps flour
2 egg yolks
½ tsp dried thyme
1 egg white
For the Pastry:
150g/5oz butter
350g/11oz flour
Salt
1 egg yolk, lightly beaten
8-10 tbsps iced water

Preparation time:
2½ hours
Baking time:
1 hour

Nutritional value:
Analysis per serving, approx:
• 2600kJ/620kcal
• 35g protein
• 44g fat
• 24g carbohydrate

First make the pastry dough. Dice the butter. Sift the flour and a pinch of salt onto a clean work surface, and make a hollow in the centre. Distribute the butter around the edge of the flour and pour the egg yolk and water into the hollow. Mix together with your fingers, pulling from the edges into the centre until the dough forms a ball. Place in a bowl, cover, and set aside to rest in the refrigerator. • Make the filling. Place the water in a large pan with a pinch of salt, and bring to the boil. Wash the duck and the giblets and reserve the liver. Add the duck and the remaining giblets to the boiling water. Lower the heat, and simmer for 30

minutes, skimming frequently.
• Peel and halve the onion.
Stud 1 half of the onion with
the cloves. Add both onion
halves, the cloves, bouquet
garni and bay leaf to the pan,
and simmer for a further 1
hour. • Remove the duck
from the pan and set aside to
cool. Strain the stock, and set
aside to cool. • Skim off the fat
and reserve 250ml/8fl oz of
stock. Skin the duck and cut
the meat from the bones.
Finely chop the duck meat. •
Finely dice the duck liver.
Finely chop the mushrooms. •
Melt 50g/2oz of the butter,
and fry the liver and the
mushrooms until lightly
browned. Stir in the flour, and
cook, stirring constantly, for 3
minutes or until golden.
Gradually stir in the reserved
stock, and bring to the boil,
stirring constantly. Lower the
heat and cook, stirring
constantly, for 5 minutes.
Remove from the heat and
allow to cool slightly. Stir in 1
egg yolk and the thyme, and
season to taste with salt and
pepper. Add the duck meat. •
Whisk the egg white until stiff,
and fold into the filling. •
Grease a 26cm/8-inch flan tin
or dish with the remaining
butter. • Halve the dough and
roll out 1 piece on a lightly-
floured work surface until it is
a little larger than the flan tin.
Line the tin with the dough,
easing it carefully with your
fingers. Prick the base with a
fork. • Spoon in the filling and
smooth the top. Dampen the
edges of the dough with water.
Roll out the other half of the
dough until it is a little larger
than the flan tin. Lift the
dough over the filling. Press
the edges together firmly to
seal, and trim to fit. Make a
decorative edging using a fork
and prick the top. Make a
decorative diamond pattern, if
liked. • Beat the remaining egg
yolk, and brush over the top of
the pie. • Bake in a preheated
oven at 220°C/425°F/gas
mark 7 for 1 hour. Allow to
cool in the tin.

Chicken Strudel

To serve 8:

2 x 1kg/2¼ lb chickens, with giblets
100g/4oz rindless smoked bacon
1 tsp dried thyme
1 tsp dried sage
Salt and freshly ground white pepper
100g/4oz mushrooms
10 large savoy cabbage leaves
2 eggs
2 tbsps finely chopped fresh parsley
125ml/4fl oz double cream
15g/½oz butter

For the Pastry:

300g/10oz flour
1 egg
Salt
125ml/4fl oz lukewarm water
1 tbsp sunflower oil
2 tbsps flour
75g/3oz butter

Preparation time:
1½ hours
Baking time:
30 minutes
Nutritional value:
Analysis per serving, approx:
• 3000kJ/710kcal
• 61g protein
• 40g fat
• 30g carbohydrate

Skin the chickens and remove the breasts. Cut the remaining meat from the bones and dice. • Trim the chicken livers. Wash, pat dry and dice. • Cut the bacon into 1cm/½-inch wide strips. Place the chicken and the bacon on a plate, sprinkle over the thyme and sage, and season to taste with salt and pepper. Set aside in the refrigerator for 30 minutes. • Finely slice the

mushrooms. Wash the cabbage leaves, pat dry and remove the stalks. • Make the pastry. Sift the flour onto a clean work surface. Add the egg, ¼ tsp salt and half the water, and knead into a smooth dough. Add a little more water, if necessary. The dough should be smooth and shiny. Shape the dough into a ball, brush with the oil, cover and set aside to rest for 30 minutes. • Put the chicken meat, apart from the breast, through a mincer twice, on its finest setting. • Put the minced meat in a bowl over ice cubes. Stir in the eggs, parsley and cream. Season to taste with salt and pepper. Cover and set aside over the ice for 30 minutes. • Cut the chicken breast into 2cm/¾-inch wide strips. Melt the butter, and stir-fry the chicken breast and the livers and over a high heat for 2 minutes. Drain on kitchen paper and set aside. • Roll out the dough on a lightly floured work surface to a large, paper-thin square. Trim off any thick edges. Melt 50g/2oz of the butter and brush over the dough. • Spread half the chicken stuffing over the cabbage leaves. Place the strips of breast meat and the diced liver in the centre. Cover with the remaining stuffing. Place everything on the dough and roll up. • Shape the pastry roll into a horse shoe and lay on the baking sheet. Melt the remaining butter, and brush half of it over the pastry roll. • Bake in a preheated oven at 200°C/400°F/gas mark 6 for 30 minutes. • During the baking time, brush the pastry roll frequently with the remaining melted butter. • Cut the chicken strudel into 16 equal portions, and serve hot with a colourful mixed salad.

Mango and Turkey Salad

125g/5oz long-grain brown rice
475ml/15fl oz water
1 tsp whole cardamom seeds
½ tsp curry powder
Salt and freshly ground white pepper
3 x 150g/5oz turkey escalopes
Juice ½ lemon
1 x 300g/10oz ripe mango
2 tbsps crème fraîche
2 tbsps sesame oil
4 tbsps chicken stock
2 tbsps finely chopped fresh dill
4 tbsps sesame seeds
Lettuce leaves and dill, to garnish

Preparation time:
50 minutes
Nutritional value:
Analysis per serving, approx:
• 1800kJ/430kcal
• 25g protein
• 21g fat
• 37g carbohydrate

Wash the rice under cold running water. Place in a pan with the water, cardamom seeds and half the curry powder, and season to taste with salt. Bring to the boil. Stir once, reduce the heat, cover and simmer for 25 minutes. • Wash the turkey escalopes and pat dry. Sprinkle over half the lemon juice, and season to taste with pepper. • Place the escalopes on the rice, cover and cook for a further 5 minutes. Turn the escalopes, cover and cook for a further 5 minutes. • Remove the escalopes and set aside to cool. Drain the rice and set aside to cool. Cut the escalopes into strips. • Peel the mango. Chop half and slice the other half. • Mix the rice with the remaining lemon juice, remaining curry powder, turkey strips, chopped mango, crème fraîche, sesame oil, stock and dill, and season to taste with salt. • Dry-fry the sesame seeds until they change colour and give off a pleasant smell. • Arrange the rice salad on a dish and sprinkle over the sesame seeds. Garnish with lettuce, mango and dill.

Indian Rice Salad

125g/5oz long-grain brown rice
600ml/1 pint water
1 tsp vegetable stock granules
200g/7oz cooked chicken
2 bananas
1 tsp lemon juice
150ml/5fl oz natural set yogurt
1 tbsp crème fraîche
1 tbsp sesame oil
2 tbsps white wine vinegar
125ml/4fl oz chicken stock
1 small red pepper
1 onion
150g/5oz fresh, peeled pineapple
1-2 tsps freshly grated root ginger
1 tsp curry powder
Lemon balm sprig
Lettuce leaves
1 very small yellow pepper

Preparation time:
45 minutes
Nutritional value:
Analysis per serving, approx:
• 1300kJ/310kcal
• 15g protein
• 8g fat
• 45g carbohydrate

Wash the rice. Place in a saucepan with the water and stock granules, and bring to the boil. Stir, reduce the heat, cover and simmer for 35 minutes. • Cut the chicken into strips. Peel the bananas. Slice 1 banana and sprinkle with the lemon juice. Mash the other banana, and mix with the yogurt, crème fraîche, oil, vinegar and chicken stock. • Halve, seed and wash the red pepper. Chop most of the pepper and cut the rest into matchstick strips for the garnish. Peel and finely chop the onion. Finely dice the pineapple. Wash the lemon balm and pat dry. Coarsely chop half, and reserve the other half for the garnish. • Mix together the rice, chicken, diced pineapple, sliced banana, onion and chopped red pepper. Stir in the banana dressing, ginger, curry powder and chopped lemon balm, and season. Halve, seed and wash the yellow pepper. Cut into matchstick strips. • Garnish the rice salad with lettuce, pepper strips, lemon balm leaves, pineapple and banana.

Potato Salad with Turkey Breast

750g/1½ lbs waxy potatoes
250ml/8fl oz chicken stock
2 red onions
2 ripe avocado pears
Salt and freshly ground black pepper
3-4 tbsps white wine vinegar
2 tbsps sunflower oil
300g/10oz smoked turkey breast
2 tbsps chopped fresh dill

Preparation time:
40 minutes
Cooking time:
30 minutes
Nutritional value:
Analysis per serving, approx:
• 2100kJ/500kcal
• 24g protein
• 28g fat
• 37g carbohydrate

Scrub the potatoes, place in a saucepan, cover with water and bring to the boil. Cover and cook for 30 minutes. • Bring the stock to the boil. • Peel, quarter and thinly slice the onions. • Peel, halve and stone the avocado pears. Cut in half lengthways once more and slice. • Drain the potatoes, rinse in cold water, peel and dice. Mix together the potatoes and hot chicken stock, and season to taste with pepper. Gently stir in the onion and avocado pears. Pour over the vinegar and oil, and season to taste with salt. Toss lightly. • Dice the turkey breast. Season the salad with salt to taste and add the turkey breast. Toss lightly. • Serve sprinkled with the dill.

Duck Salad

75g/3oz *whole* oats
475ml/15fl *oz* chicken stock
400g/14oz *savoy* cabbage
1l/1¾ pints *water*
Salt and *freshly* ground black
pepper
1 red onion
400g/14oz *cooked* duck fillet
1 tbsp *sunflower* oil
2 tbsps red *wine* vinegar
1 tsp *Worcester*shire sauce

Preparation time:
50 minutes
Nutritional value:
Analysis per serving, approx:
• 1800kJ/430kcal
• 26g protein
• 22g fat
• 30g carbohydrate

Place the oats and chicken stock in a pan, and bring to the boil. Boil for 5 minutes, lower the heat, cover and simmer gently for 40 minutes. • Meanwhile, wash the cabbage, discarding the stalk and tough outer leaves. Shake dry and finely shred. Place the water in a pan and bring to the boil. Add a pinch of salt and blanch the cabbage for 5 minutes. Drain. • Peel, quarter and thinly slice the onion. Thinly slice the duck fillet. • Drain the cooked oats, reserving a little of the stock. • Mix together the warm oats and the cabbage. Pour over the oil, vinegar and Worcestershire sauce, and season to taste with pepper. Mix thoroughly. Add a little of the reserved chicken stock, if liked. • Arrange the oat salad on a serving dish and top with the onion and duck slices.

Index